· Cooking for Today ·

CLASSIC CAKES

·*Cooking for Today*·

CLASSIC CAKES

ROSEMARY WADEY

SIENA

A Siena Book
Siena is an imprint of Parragon Books

First published in Great Britain in 1996 by
Parragon Book Service Ltd
Unit 13–17
Avonbridge Trading Estate
Atlantic Road
Avonmouth
Bristol BS11 9QD

ISBN 0-7525-1520-9

Produced by Haldane Mason, London

Printed in Italy

Acknowledgements:
Art Direction: Ron Samuels
Editor: Joanna Swinnerton
Series Design: Pedro & Frances Prá-Lopez/Kingfisher Design
Page Design: Somewhere Creative
Photography: Joff Lee
Styling: John Lee Studios
Home Economist: Rosemary Wadey

Photographs on pages 6, 20, 34, 48 & 62 reproduced by permission of
ZEFA Picture Library (UK) Ltd.

Note:
*Cup measurements in this book are for American cups. Tablespoons are assumed to be 15 ml.
Unless otherwise stated, milk is assumed to be full-fat, eggs are standard size 3 and pepper
is freshly ground black pepper.*

Contents

CHAPTER ONE

Sponge Cakes

A book of classic cakes must surely begin with the favourites, such as Victoria Sandwich (Sponge Layer Cake) and Madeira (Pound) Cake, together with some of the very many variations on these two basic cakes. Following hot on their heels comes the whisked Chocolate Roulade, so versatile and well loved – with a filling to suit every occasion.

The secret of success with these cakes is to make sure the initial creaming process is continued until the mixture is more than light and fluffy and pale in colour – do not cut down on this important stage, whether creaming by hand, with a hand-held electric mixer or in a large mixer, or your cakes will never rise well and achieve the lightness everyone loves. The same applies to the whisked cakes; make sure the mixture is really thick and the whisk leaves a heavy trail before proceeding.

These cakes can be filled simply with jam or lemon curd, or have a variety of butter cream fillings and toppings; fresh cream can turn the cake into a dessert; marzipan can enclose the whole cake to create a Battenburg, or a sugar and lemon juice topping can be added to the warm cake to transform it into something almost out of this world.

Opposite: Choosing the freshest basic ingredients is the first step towards baking the perfect cake.

STEP 1

STEP 4

STEP 5

STEP 6

VICTORIA SANDWICH (SPONGE LAYER CAKE)

Probably the best-known sponge cake of all and most popular in both its natural flavour or one of the many variations.

MAKES 18 CM/7 INCH CAKE

125 g/4 oz/¹/₂ cup butter or margarine
125 g/4 oz/¹/₂ cup caster (superfine) sugar
2 eggs, beaten
125 g/4 oz/1 cup self-raising flour, sifted
1 tbsp water
few drops of vanilla or other flavouring
    (extract)
5–6 tbsp raspberry or other jam
icing (confectioners') or caster (superfine)
    sugar for dredging

1 Grease 2 round sandwich tins (layer pans) 18 cm/7 inches across, and line the bases with non-stick baking parchment.

2 Cream the fat and sugar together until very light, fluffy and pale.

3 Beat in the eggs, one at a time, following each with a spoonful of the sifted flour.

4 Fold in the remaining flour, followed by the water and vanilla flavouring (extract).

5 Divide the mixture equally between the tins (pans) and level the tops. Bake in a preheated oven at 190°C/

375°F/Gas Mark 5 for about 20 minutes, or until well risen, golden brown and firm to the touch. Invert on to a wire rack and leave to cool.

6 When cold, sandwich the 2 cakes together with jam and dredge the top with sifted icing (confectioners') sugar or caster (superfine) sugar. Transfer to a plate to serve.

VARIATIONS

Lemon or orange: Add the grated rind of 1–2 lemons or oranges and replace the water with lemon or orange juice. Fill with butter cream (see page 76).

Coffee: Replace the water with 1 tablespoon coffee flavouring (extract) or very strong black coffee. Fill with butter cream (see page 76).

Chocolate: Replace 25–30 g/³/₄–1 oz/ 3–4 tablespoons flour with sifted cocoa powder and add ¹/₄ teaspoon baking powder. Fill with butter cream (see page 76).

STEP 3

STEP 4

STEP 6

STEP 7

CHOCOLATE ROULADE

A rich whisked mixture of eggs, sugar and dark chocolate to roll up with a filling of alcohol-flavoured fresh cream dredged with icing (confectioners') sugar.

MAKES 25 CM/10 INCH ROULADE

175 g/6 oz/6 squares dark chocolate
5 eggs, separated
175 g/6 oz/³/₄ cup caster (superfine) sugar
few drops of vanilla flavouring (extract)
icing (confectioners') sugar
coarsely grated chocolate or miniature
    chocolate curls to decorate (see page 79)

CREAM FILLING:
300 ml/¹/₂ pint/1¹/₄ cups double (heavy)
    cream
2–4 tbsp rum, brandy or liqueur

1 Melt the chocolate in a bowl over a saucepan of gently simmering water, or in a microwave oven on Full Power for about 45 seconds. Stir until smooth.

2 Line a Swiss (jelly) roll tin (pan), about 30 × 25 cm/12 × 10 inches, with non-stick baking parchment. Whisk the egg yolks and sugar until very thick and creamy. Fold the melted chocolate through the egg yolk mixture with the vanilla.

3 Whisk the egg whites until very stiff and dry, and fold through the egg yolk mixture until blended. Spread

out evenly in the prepared tin (pan), especially into the corners.

4 Bake in a preheated oven at 190°C/ 375°F/Gas Mark 5 for about 15–20 minutes, or until firm and crusty on top. Sprinkle a sheet of baking parchment very liberally with the sifted icing (confectioners') sugar. Invert the cake on to the paper and leave to cool slightly; then lay a damp tea towel (dish cloth) over the cake and leave until cold.

5 To make the filling, whip the cream until thick but not too stiff and fold in the alcohol. Put about 3–4 tablespoons of the filling into a piping bag fitted with a large star nozzle (tip).

6 Peel the lining paper off the cake and spread evenly with the cream.

7 Roll up the cake carefully with the help of the paper and transfer to a serving plate. Pipe a line of the filling along the top of the cake and decorate with grated chocolate or chocolate curls.

STEP 4

STEP 5

STEP 5

STEP 6

BATTENBURG CAKE

Battenburg or 'window cake', as it is often affectionately known, is made from basic Victoria Sandwich (Layer Sponge) cake mixture in two colours, cut into blocks and wrapped in marzipan to give a chequered effect when cut.

MAKES 28 CM/11 INCH CAKE

175 g/6 oz/³/₄ cup butter or margarine
175 g/6 oz/1 cup light soft brown sugar
3 eggs
175 g/6 oz/1¹/₂ cups self-raising flour, sifted
1 tbsp water
pink food colouring
few drops of raspberry flavouring (extract)
* or ¹/₂ tsp triple-strength rose water*
1 tbsp sifted cocoa powder
about 150 g/5 oz/¹/₂ cup apricot jam, sieved
* (strained)*
225 g/8 oz marzipan (see page 78)
granulated sugar

1 Grease a rectangular tin (pan), about 28 × 18 × 4 cm/11 × 7 × 1¹/₂ inches, and line with non-stick baking parchment. Divide the tin (pan) in half across the centre with a double thickness of foil.

2 Cream the fat and sugar together until light, fluffy and pale. Beat in the eggs one at a time, following each with a spoonful of flour. Fold in the remaining flour, followed by the water.

3 Transfer half the mixture to another bowl. Colour one half with pink food colouring and raspberry

flavouring (extract) or rose water. Add the cocoa powder to the other half.

4 Spoon the chocolate mixture into one part of the tin (pan) and the pink mixture into the other, and level the top. Bake in a preheated oven at 190°C/375°F/Gas Mark 5 for about 25 minutes, or until well risen and firm to the touch. Invert on to a wire rack to cool. Trim the cakes and cut in half lengthways.

5 Spread the top of one pink and one brown piece of cake with apricot jam and top with pieces of the contrasting colour. Spread the sides of 1 double layer with jam and stick the 2 pieces together to give the chequered effect. Use the remaining jam to brush around the outside of the cake.

6 Roll out the marzipan on baking parchment, to an oblong large enough to enclose the whole cake. Position the cake in the centre and wrap the marzipan around the sides to enclose it; trim neatly. Crimp or decorate the outer edges of the marzipan and mark a criss-cross pattern on top with a sharp knife. Sprinkle with a little granulated sugar and leave to set.

ORANGE CREAM CAKE

An orange-flavoured cake set in the baking tin (pan) with an orange mousse filling and decorated with a layer of marmalade and butter cream.

STEP 3

STEP 4

STEP 5

MAKES 23 CM/9 INCH ROUND CAKE

250 g/8 oz/1 cup butter or margarine
250 g/8 oz/1 cup caster (superfine) sugar
4 eggs
250 g/8 oz/2 cups self-raising flour, sifted
grated rind of 1 large or 2 small oranges
1 tbsp orange juice

MOUSSE:
1 egg
90 g/3 oz/¹/₃ cup caster (superfine) sugar
grated rind of 1 orange
125 g/4 oz/¹/₂ cup low-fat soft cheese
2 tsp powdered gelatine
2 tbsp orange juice

TOPPING:
4 tbsp orange shred marmalade
60 g/2 oz/¹/₄ cup butter
125 g/4 oz/scant 1 cup icing
(confectioners') sugar, sifted
1 tsp orange flower water
jellied orange slices to decorate

1 Grease and line a 23 cm/9 inch round springform cake tin (pan) with non-stick baking parchment. Make up the cake mixture as for Victoria Sandwich (Sponge Layer Cake) (see page 8), adding the orange rind and juice instead of water.

2 Transfer to the tin (pan), level the top and bake in a preheated oven at 180°C/350°F/Gas Mark 4 for about 45 minutes, or until well risen, golden brown and firm to the touch. Invert on to a wire rack and leave to cool.

3 When cold, peel off the paper and cut the cake in half horizontally. Line the cake tin (pan) with fresh non-stick baking parchment and place the bottom half of the cake in the tin (pan).

4 For the mousse, whisk the egg and sugar together until thick. Whisk in the orange rind, then the soft cheese. Dissolve the gelatine in the orange juice over a saucepan of simmering water until clear.

5 Leave to cool slightly and stir into the cheese mixture. When almost setting, spread over the cake and press the top layer in place. Chill until set.

6 Remove the cake from the tin (pan). Spread marmalade over the top. Cream the butter and sugar together and add the orange flower water. Put into a piping bag with a large star nozzle (tip) and pipe shells around the top of the cake. Decorate with orange slices.

STEP 5

STEP 3

STEP 4

STEP 5

STEP 6

MARBLED CAKE

Chocolate, orange and vanilla are swirled together to give an attractive appearance and a delicious blend of flavours.

MAKES 20 CM/8 INCH SQUARE OR
23 CM/9 INCH ROUND CAKE

60 g/2 oz/2 squares dark chocolate
1 tbsp water
175 g/6 oz/³/₄ cup butter or margarine
175 g/6 oz/³/₄ cup caster (superfine) sugar
275 g/9 oz/2¹/₄ cups plain (all-purpose)
    flour
2 tsp baking powder
3 eggs
2 tbsp milk or water
grated rind of 1 orange
1 tsp orange flower water
few drops of orange food colouring
1 tsp vanilla flavouring (extract)
icing (confectioners') sugar for dredging

1 Line a 20 cm/8 inch square or 23 cm/9 inch round cake tin (pan) with non-stick baking parchment. Melt the chocolate and water in a bowl over simmering water or in a microwave oven set on Full Power for about 45 seconds.

2 Cream the fat and sugar together until very light and fluffy. Sift the flour and baking powder together. Beat the eggs one at a time into the sugar mixture, following each with a spoonful of the flour, then fold in the remainder with the milk or water.

3 Put one third of the mixture into another bowl and beat in the orange rind, orange flower water and colouring. Add the flavouring (extract) to the remaining mixture, then transfer half to another bowl and beat in the melted chocolate.

4 Place large spoonfuls of the 3 cake mixtures alternately into the cake tin (pan).

5 Cut through the mixture with a knife several times to swirl the colours and flavours together, then level the top. Bake in a preheated oven at 180°C/350°F/Gas Mark 4 for about an hour, or until well risen and firm to the touch.

6 Leave to cool slightly in the tin (pan), then invert on to a wire rack to cool completely. Before serving dredge the top with sifted icing (confectioners') sugar.

NOTE

This cake can be kept frozen for up to 3 months.

MADEIRA (POUND) CAKE

This is a very traditional cake flavoured with lemon, which can be served plain or covered in marzipan and icing (frosting) for a simple celebration cake. It will keep for up to two weeks.

STEP 2

STEP 3

STEP 5

STEP 6

MAKES 18 CM/7 INCH ROUND OR
SQUARE CAKE

175 g/6 oz/³/₄ cup butter
175 g/6 oz/³/₄ cup caster (superfine) sugar
175 g/6 oz/1¹/₂ cups self-raising flour
90 g/3 oz/³/₄ cup plain (all-purpose) flour
3 eggs
grated rind of 1–2 lemons
1 tbsp lemon juice
thin slices of candied citron peel (optional)

1 Grease an 18 cm/7 inch round or square deep cake tin (pan) or a 900 g/2 lb loaf tin (pan) and line the base with non-stick baking parchment.

2 Beat the butter until soft and add the sugar. Cream together until very light and fluffy and pale in colour.

3 Sift the flours together. Beat the eggs into the creamed mixture one at a time, following each with a tablespoonful of the flour.

4 Fold the remaining flour into the cake mixture, followed by the lemon rind and juice. The mixture should be soft but not sloppy or pourable.

5 Transfer to the prepared tin (pan), level the top, and add a few slices of citron peel, if using.

6 Bake in a preheated oven at 160°C/325°F/Gas Mark 3 for about 1¹/₄ hours, or until well risen, firm and browned. Test by inserting a skewer in the cake; it should come out clean if the cake is cooked.

7 Leave to cool in the tin (pan) for about 5 minutes, then invert on to a wire rack and leave until cold. Peel off the paper and store the cake in an airtight container until required.

VARIATIONS

For an iced (frosted) cake, do not add the citron peel.

Lemon Frosted Topping: Blend sufficient lemon juice (1–2 tablespoons) with 60 g/2 oz/¹/₄ cup caster (superfine) sugar and spread over the hot cake. It will crystallize as the cake cools.

Orange Madeira (Pound) Cake: Replace the lemon rind with orange rind but keep the lemon juice.

Coffee Walnut Cake: Omit lemon rind and replace lemon juice with coffee flavouring (extract); add 60 g/2 oz/¹/₂ cup chopped walnuts.

CHAPTER TWO

Small Cakes

No book of classic cake recipes would be complete without a chapter on small or individual cakes. The variety is huge and ranges from tartlets and sponge cakes to meringues; some are baked individually, but many are baked in slabs, which are then cut into squares or fingers (bars).

Some small cakes are coated in a variety of icings (frostings) such as glacé, butter cream, or even melted chocolate, while others are merely dredged with sifted icing (confectioners') sugar or sprinkled with caster (superfine) sugar.

Small cakes are ideal for serving at any time with a cup of tea or coffee. They are also very popular at buffet parties, or to feed hungry children, and ideal to make for a cake stall at a fund-raising event. Many of these small cakes freeze well, either ready to serve or before finishing the decoration; being small, they can be removed a few at a time, and they thaw very quickly.

Master the art of choux paste to produce delicious éclairs and serve them oozing with whipped cream; serve Eccles Cakes and Maids of Honour, both pastry-based; and make pretty Butterfly Cakes and Mocha Boxes or Brownies, all ideal for chocoholics!

Opposite: *An attractive array of small cakes will suit any occasion, and can be fun to make and decorate.*

STEP 2

STEP 3

STEP 4

STEP 6

CHOCOLATE ECLAIRS

Everyone's favourites – these light choux fingers (shells) are filled with cream and topped with chocolate or coffee icing (frosting).

MAKES 12–14

CHOUX PASTE:
75 g/2¹/₂ oz/¹/₂ cup plus 2 tbsp plain
* (all-purpose) flour*
pinch of salt
60 g/2 oz/¹/₄ cup butter or margarine
150 ml/¹/₄ pint/²/₃ cup water
2 eggs, beaten

FILLING:
300 ml/¹/₂ pint/1¹/₄ cups double (heavy)
* cream or 1 quantity of Pastry Cream (see*
* page 78)*

TOPPING:
125 g/4 oz/4 squares dark chocolate
* or white chocolate*

1 Grease 2 baking sheets. Sift the flour and salt together. Put the butter or margarine and water into a saucepan and heat gently until the fat melts, then bring to the boil.

2 Add the flour all at once and beat vigorously until the paste is smooth and forms a ball that leaves the sides of the saucepan clean. Remove from the heat and spread the paste out over the base of the saucepan. Leave to cool for about 10 minutes.

3 Beat in the eggs gradually until the mixture is smooth, glossy and gives a piping consistency. It may not need quite all of the egg. A hand-held electric mixer is ideal for this.

4 Put the choux paste into a piping bag fitted with a plain 2 cm/³/₄ inch nozzle (tip) and pipe in straight lines about 6 cm/2¹/₂ inches long, spaced well apart on the baking sheets. Cut the ends of the paste from the nozzle (tip).

5 Bake in a preheated oven at 220°C/ 425°F/Gas Mark 7 for about 20–25 minutes, or until well risen, firm and a pale golden brown. Make a slit in the side of each éclair to let the steam escape, and return to the oven to dry out for a few minutes. Transfer to a wire rack to cool.

6 Whip the cream until stiff and use to fill each éclair, or use the pastry cream to fill the éclairs. Melt the chocolate in a bowl over simmering water, or in a microwave oven set on Full Power for 45 seconds. Remove from the heat and leave to cool until just beginning to thicken. Dip the top of each éclair into the chocolate, or spread with a palette knife (spatula). Leave to set.

STEP 2

STEP 3

STEP 4

STEP 5

AMERICAN BROWNIES

These are the moist and slightly chewy chocolate and nut American specialities which are now popular everywhere.

MAKES 20

125 g/4 oz/4 squares dark chocolate,
 broken into pieces
150 g/5 oz/²⁄₃ cup butter or margarine
350 g/12 oz/1¹⁄₂ cups caster (superfine)
 sugar
¹⁄₂ tsp vanilla flavouring (extract)
4 eggs, beaten
150 g/5 oz/1¹⁄₄ cups self-raising flour
90 g/3 oz/³⁄₄ cup pecans, walnuts, hazelnuts
 or almonds, chopped
60 g/2 oz/¹⁄₃ cup raisins
icing (confectioners') sugar for dredging

1 Line a rectangular tin (pan), about 28 × 18 × 4 cm/11 × 7 × 1¹⁄₂ inches, with non-stick baking parchment.

2 Put the chocolate and butter or margarine into a heatproof bowl and either place over a saucepan of gently simmering water and heat until melted, or melt in a microwave oven set on Full Power for about 1 minute. Stir until quite smooth.

3 Remove from the heat and beat in the sugar and flavouring (extract) until smooth, followed by the eggs.

4 Sift the flour and fold through the mixture, followed by the chopped nuts and raisins.

5 Pour into the prepared tin (pan) and bake in a preheated oven at 180°C/350°F/Gas Mark 4 for about 45–50 minutes, or until well risen, firm to the touch, and just beginning to shrink away from the sides of the tin (pan). Leave to cool in the tin (pan).

6 Dredge heavily with sifted icing (confectioners') sugar and cut into 20 squares or fingers (bars). Store in an airtight container. The brownies will keep well for a week.

NOTE

Brownies can be frozen successfully` for up to 3 months, but it is best to add the icing (confectioners') sugar after thawing.

If preferred, the Brownies may be topped with chocolate butter cream (see page 79) sprinkled with grated dark or white chocolate; or simply be swirled with melted dark or white chocolate.

STEP 3

STEP 4

STEP 5

STEP 7

ECCLES CAKES

Crisp and buttery puff pastry circles with a spiced currant and mixed peel filling.

MAKES 8–10

300 g/10 oz puff pastry, thawed if frozen
beaten egg white for glazing
caster (superfine) sugar for dredging

FILLING:
30 g/1 oz/2 tbsp butter, softened
30 g/1 oz/3 tbsp dark soft brown sugar
30 g/1 oz/3 tbsp chopped mixed
  (candied) peel
125 g/4 oz/²/₃ cup currants
generous pinch of grated nutmeg
¹/₄–¹/₂ tsp mixed (apple pie) spice
grated rind of ¹/₂–1 orange (optional)

1 To make the filling, beat the butter until soft, then work in the sugar, peel, currants, nutmeg, spice and orange rind, if using.

2 Roll out the pastry thinly on a lightly floured work surface (counter) and cut into circles of about 13 cm/5¹/₂ inches – a saucer is a good guide.

3 Put a tablespoonful of the filling in the centre of each circle.

4 Dampen the edges of the pastry and gather together like a bag, pressing the edges well together to seal.

5 Turn each one over and, keeping the round shape, flatten gently with a rolling pin until the currants just begin to show through.

6 Brush each one liberally with egg white and dredge with sugar.

7 Transfer to a lightly greased baking sheet and make 2–3 small cuts in the top of each one. Bake in a preheated oven at 220°C/425°F/Gas Mark 7 for about 10–15 minutes, or until well puffed up and golden brown. Transfer to a wire rack to cool. Store in an airtight container. They will keep for up to a week; or freeze for up to 2 months.

PUFF PASTRY

Puff pastry can be bought either fresh or frozen. Thaw frozen pastry at room temperature for about 2 hours and use within 24 hours. Use fresh puff pastry within 48 hours.

BUTTERFLY CAKES

Sponge cakes of any flavour baked in paper cases with 'butterfly wings' and decorated with butter cream.

STEP 2

MAKES 16

1 quantity Victoria Sandwich (Sponge Layer
    Cake) mixture (see page 8)
grated rind of 1 orange or lemon or 2 tbsp
    sifted cocoa powder or 1 tbsp coffee
    flavouring (extract)
icing (confectioners') sugar for dredging

BUTTER CREAM:
125 g/4 oz/¹/₂ cup butter or margarine
250 g/8 oz/1³/₄ cups icing (confectioners')
    sugar, sifted
1–2 tbsp coffee flavouring (extract) or 2
    tbsp sifted cocoa powder or grated rind of
    1 orange or lemon
1–2 tbsp milk, lemon or orange juice

1 Line 16 patty tins (muffin pans)
    with paper cake cases or grease
them thoroughly.

2 Make up the cake mixture using
    one of the flavourings and divide
between the paper cases or patty tins
(muffin pans).

3 Bake in a preheated oven at
    190°C/375°F/Gas Mark 5 for
about 15–20 minutes, or until well risen
and just firm to the touch. Place on a
wire rack and leave to cool.

4 Make up the butter cream in a
    flavour to complement the sponge
mixture and put into a piping bag fitted
with a small star nozzle (tip).

5 Cut a small piece out of the top of
    each bun, leaving about 1 cm/¹/₂
inch all round the top surface uncut; and
cut the removed piece in half to form the
'wings'.

6 Pipe a whirl of butter cream to fill
    the hole which has been cut out of
each bun. Place the 'wings' in position,
tilting them up at the edges. Either leave
the 'wings' as they are or pipe a little
butter cream between and around them.
Dredge lightly with icing (confectioners')
sugar before serving.

STEP 3

STEP 5

NOTE

These small cakes can be kept frozen for
up to 3 months.

STEP 6

MOCHA BOXES

A delicious coffee and chocolate-flavoured cake and butter cream for these squares of cake enclosed in chocolate cases.

STEP 3

STEP 4

STEP 5

STEP 6

MAKES 16

350 g/12 oz/12 squares dark cake-covering
  chocolate
16 chocolate matchsticks to decorate

CAKE MIXTURE:
175 g/6 oz/³/₄ cup butter or margarine
175 g/6 oz/1 cup light soft brown sugar
3 eggs
175 g/6 oz/1¹/₂ cups self-raising flour
90 g/3 oz/³/₄ cup plain (all-purpose) flour
1 tbsp sifted cocoa powder
1 tbsp coffee flavouring (extract)

MOCHA BUTTER CREAM:
125 g/4 oz/¹/₂ cup butter or margarine
250 g/8 oz/1³/₄ cups icing (confectioners')
  sugar, sifted
1 tbsp sifted cocoa powder
2–3 tsp coffee flavouring (extract)

1 Line a 20 cm/8 inch deep square cake tin (pan) with non-stick baking parchment. Make up the cake as on page 18, but use the cake mixture ingredients above. Put into the tin (pan), level the top and bake in a preheated oven at 160°C/325°F/Gas Mark 3 for about 1–1¹/₄ hours, until well risen and firm and a skewer inserted in the centre comes out clean. Invert on a wire rack.

2 When cool, trim and level the cake and cut into 16 even-sized squares (a little less than 5 cm/2 inches each).

3 Melt the chocolate in a bowl over a saucepan of simmering water or in a microwave oven set on Full Power for 45 seconds, then spread out thinly on a sheet of baking parchment to a square of 40 cm/16 inches. Pick up one corner of the paper and shake lightly to level the chocolate. Leave until barely set.

4 Using a sharp knife and a ruler, cut the chocolate into 64 × 5 cm/2 inch squares. Chill until completely set.

5 For the butter cream, cream the butter, sugar, cocoa powder and coffee flavouring (extract) to give a spreading consistency. Mask the sides and top of each cake square with butter cream and put the remainder into a piping bag with a large star nozzle (tip).

6 Press a square of chocolate to each side of the squares, then pipe a large whirl of butter cream on top of each box. Decorate with 2 or 3 chocolate matchsticks.

STEP 2

STEP 3

STEP 4

STEP 6

MAIDS OF HONOUR

Traditional small curd tartlets flavoured with brandy, almonds and currants which originated at the court of Henry VIII at Hampton Court Palace and became favourites with the queen's Maids of Honour. If you like, you can top them with slices of fresh fruit and whipped cream.

MAKES ABOUT 20

SHORTCRUST (PLAIN) PASTRY:
175 g/6 oz/1½ cups plain (all-purpose) flour
pinch of salt
45 g/1½ oz/3 tbsp butter or block margarine
45 g/1½ oz/3 tbsp lard (shortening) or white vegetable fat
about 4 tbsp cold water to mix

FILLING:
150 g/5 oz/⅔ cup curd (smooth cottage) cheese
90 g/3 oz/⅓ cup softened butter
2 eggs
1 tbsp brandy
30 g/1 oz/¼ cup blanched flaked (slivered) almonds, chopped
few drops of almond flavouring (extract) (optional)
2 tbsp caster (superfine) sugar
60 g/2 oz/⅓ cup currants

1 To make the pastry dough, sift the flour and salt into a bowl and rub in the fat until the mixture resembles fine breadcrumbs. Add sufficient cold water to mix to a pliable dough, knead lightly and wrap in clingfilm (plastic wrap) or foil; chill while making the filling.

2 To make the filling, work the curd (smooth cottage) cheese and butter together carefully. Whisk the eggs and brandy together, and work into the cheese mixture with the almonds, almond flavouring (extract) and sugar.

3 Roll out the pastry thinly on a lightly floured work surface (counter) and cut into about 20 fluted circles about 7 cm/3 inches in diameter. Place each circle carefully in a patty tin (muffin pan).

4 Divide the cheese mixture between the pastry cases and then sprinkle each with a few currants.

5 Bake in a preheated oven at 200°C/400°F/Gas Mark 6 for about 15–20 minutes, or until well risen and lightly browned.

6 Transfer to a wire rack and leave to cool. Before serving, dredge each lightly with sifted icing (confectioners') sugar and decorate as you wish.

CHAPTER THREE

Fruit & Spice Cakes

Fruit and spices go hand in glove with cakes of all types, and in fact are an important part of both rich and plainer types of cake, gingerbreads and many of the small cakes too. Fruits used include raisins, sultanas (golden raisins) and currants as well as prunes and dried apricots, which need chopping before adding, but lend a superb flavour, together with cut mixed (candied) peel, glacé (candied) cherries, angelica and a wide variety of the sweeter ground spices such as cinnamon, mixed (apple pie) spice, allspice, ground or grated nutmeg, and ginger. Chopped glacé (candied) or stem ginger is also used.

And then there are fresh fruits, which can be grated and added to many cakes. These include apples, bananas and citrus fruits of all types. All the soft fruits, such as raspberries, strawberries, blackcurrants and redcurrants, as well as kiwi fruit, mangoes, pineapple and many more, add colour and flavour and contribute greatly to the attractive decoration of very many cakes.

This chapter concentrates on the lighter cakes, such as Gingerbread, spiced Kugelhupf, Polish Cheesecake, Sherry & Spice Cake, Carrot Cake and the Welsh Bara Brith, rather than the rich fruit varieties.

Opposite: *Dried fruit and aromatic spices lend an incomparable flavour to a wide range of cakes.*

STEP 2

STEP 3

STEP 4

STEP 5

BARA BRITH

This is a Welsh teatime favourite, flavoured strongly with black treacle (molasses), spice and sultanas (golden raisins) to serve in slices, plain or buttered.

MAKES 900 G/2 LB LOAF

250 g/8 oz/2 cups self-raising flour
pinch of salt
³/₄ tsp mixed (apple pie) spice
60g/2 oz/¹/₄ cup butter or margarine
60 g/2 oz/¹/₄ cup caster (superfine) sugar or
    90 g/3 oz/¹/₂ cup light soft brown sugar
grated rind of 1 lemon
125 g/4 oz/²/₃ cup sultanas (golden raisins)
1 egg, beaten
90 g/3 oz/¹/₄ cup black treacle (molasses)
120 ml/4 fl oz/¹/₂ cup milk
¹/₂ tsp bicarbonate of soda (baking soda)

1 Line a 900 g/2 lb loaf tin (pan) with non-stick baking parchment.

2 Sift the flour, salt and spice into a bowl. Add the butter or margarine and rub in finely until the mixture resembles fine breadcrumbs.

3 Add the sugar, lemon rind and sultanas (golden raisins) to the mixture and mix evenly.

4 Add the egg to the mixture, followed by the black treacle (molasses).

5 Measure the milk into a jug or cup and sprinkle in the bicarbonate of soda (baking soda). Mix well and add to the other ingredients. Mix thoroughly until well blended. Spoon into the prepared tin (pan) and level the top.

6 Bake in a preheated oven at 180°C/ 350°F/Gas Mark 4 for about 1¹/₄ hours, or until well risen, firm to the touch and a skewer inserted in the centre comes out clean. Invert on a wire rack to cool. Store wrapped in foil or in an airtight container for 24 hours before serving in slices with butter and jam, if liked.

MEASURING TREACLE (MOLASSES)

The best way to measure black treacle (molasses) or golden (light corn) syrup is to oil a bowl or measuring cup lightly, add the treacle (molasses) or syrup and it will slide out easily without sticking.

STEP 2

STEP 3

STEP 4

STEP 5

GINGERBREAD

There are so many recipes for gingerbread – most have black treacle (molasses) and brown sugar; this one also has raisins and chopped stem ginger with a touch of orange too, if liked.

MAKES 20 CM/8 INCH SQUARE CAKE

125 g/4 oz/¹⁄₃ cup black treacle (molasses)
125 g/4 oz/¹⁄₂ cup butter or margarine
125 g/4 oz/¹⁄₂ cup demerara (brown crystal) sugar
250 g/8 oz/2 cups plain (all-purpose) flour
pinch of salt
1¹⁄₂ tsp ground ginger
90 g/3 oz/¹⁄₂ cup raisins or currants
30 g/1 oz/3 tbsp stem ginger, chopped
grated rind of 1 orange (optional)
1 egg, beaten
4 tbsp milk
¹⁄₂ tsp bicarbonate of soda (baking soda)

1 Grease and line a 20 cm/8 inch square cake tin (pan) with non-stick baking parchment.

2 Measure the treacle (molasses) into a heatproof bowl, then add the butter or margarine and sugar and melt either over a saucepan of gently simmering water, or in a microwave oven set on Full Power for about 1¹⁄₂ minutes.

3 Sift the flour, salt and ground ginger into a bowl and mix in the raisins or currants, chopped ginger and orange rind, if using.

4 Add the melted mixture to the dry ingredients with the egg and 3 tablespoons of the milk and beat until smooth and evenly blended.

5 Blend the bicarbonate of soda (baking soda) with the remaining milk and add to the mixture, then beat until smooth. Pour into the prepared tin (pan). Bake in a preheated oven at 160°C/325°F/Gas Mark 3 for about 50 minutes, or until firm to the touch.

6 Invert the gingerbread carefully on to a wire rack and leave until cold. Wrap in foil or store in an airtight container for 3–4 days before cutting.

VARIATION

For a spiced orange or lemon cake, replace the ground ginger with mixed (apple pie) spice, and omit the chopped ginger, replacing it with the grated rind of 2 oranges or lemons.

STEP 3

STEP 5

STEP 6

STEP 7

CARROT CAKE

This delicious moist cake, full of carrots, apples, pecan nuts and spice with a soft cheese topping, was originally an American favourite, but is now popular in many other countries. The cake can either be left plain or dredged with icing (confectioners') sugar.

MAKES 20 CM/8 INCH ROUND CAKE

250 g/8 oz/2 cups self-raising flour
2 tsp baking powder
1 tsp ground cinnamon
150 g/5 oz/generous $^{3}/_{4}$ cup light soft brown
   sugar
125 g/4 oz/1 cup carrots
2 dessert (eating) apples, peeled and cored
60 g/2 oz/$^{1}/_{2}$ cup pecan nuts, chopped
2 eggs
150 ml/$^{1}/_{4}$ pint/$^{2}/_{3}$ cup vegetable or corn oil

TOPPING:
90 g/3 oz/$^{1}/_{3}$ cup full-fat soft cheese
90 g/3 oz/$^{1}/_{3}$ cup softened butter or
   margarine
175 g/6 oz/$1^{1}/_{3}$ cups icing (confectioners')
   sugar, sifted
grated rind of $^{1}/_{2}$–1 orange

TO DECORATE:
pecan halves
orange jelly slices

1 Grease a 20 cm/8 inch round cake tin (pan) and line with non-stick baking parchment.

2 Sift the flour, baking powder and spice into a bowl. Mix in the sugar until evenly blended.

3 Grate the carrots and apples.

4 Add the nuts, carrot and apples to the flour mixture, and mix together lightly, then make a well in the centre.

5 Add the eggs and oil, and beat well until thoroughly blended.

6 Spoon into the tin (pan) and level the top. Bake in a preheated oven at 180°C/350°F/Gas Mark 4 for about 1 hour, or until the cake is golden brown and just slightly shrinking from the sides of the tin (pan). Test by inserting a skewer in the centre of the cake; it should come out clean. Invert on to a wire rack and leave until cold.

7 To make the topping, put all the ingredients together in a bowl and beat well until smooth. Spread over the top of the cake and swirl with a round-bladed knife or palette knife (spatula). As it sets, decorate with pecan halves and orange jelly slices.

SHERRY & SPICE CAKE

The fruit is simmered in sherry before baking in a layered cake which is sandwiched together with a sherry-flavoured butter cream.

MAKES 20 CM/8 INCH SANDWICH
(LAYER) CAKE

6 tbsp sherry
175 g/6 oz/1 cup sultanas (golden raisins)
125 g/4 oz/½ cup butter or margarine
125 g/4 oz/⅔ cup light soft brown sugar
2 eggs
175 g/6 oz/1½ cups plain (all-purpose)
   flour
1 tsp bicarbonate of soda (baking soda)
½ tsp ground cloves
¼ tsp ground or grated nutmeg
½ tsp ground cinnamon
60 g/2 oz/½ cup walnuts, chopped

TO DECORATE:
1 egg yolk
1 tbsp sherry
1 quantity Butter Cream (see page 76)
icing (confectioners') sugar for dredging
walnut or pecan halves

1 Grease 2 × 20 cm/8 inch sandwich tins (layer pans) and line the bases with non-stick baking parchment. Bring the sherry, sultanas (golden raisins) and 4 tablespoons water to the boil. Cover and simmer for 15 minutes. Strain off the liquid and make it up to 5 tablespoons with cold water.

2 Cream the butter and sugar until pale and fluffy. Beat in the eggs one at a time, following each with a spoonful of flour. Sift the remaining flour with the bicarbonate of soda (baking soda) and spices, and fold into the mixture, with the cooled sultana (golden raisin) liquor.

3 Add the nuts and sultanas (golden raisins), and mix lightly. Divide between the tins (pans). Level the tops.

4 Bake in a preheated oven at 180°C/350°F/Gas Mark 4 for 25–35 minutes, until firm to the touch. Cool briefly in the tin (pan), loosen the edges and invert on to a wire rack to cool.

5 Beat the egg yolk and sherry into the butter cream. Add a little sifted icing (confectioners') sugar, if necessary. Use half to sandwich the cakes together, then sift icing (confectioners') sugar lightly over the top of the cake.

6 Place the remaining butter cream in a piping bag fitted with a large star nozzle (tip) and pipe a row of elongated shells around the top about 2.5 cm/1 inch in from the edge. Complete the decoration with pecan or walnut halves.

STEP 2

STEP 3

STEP 3

STEP 5

POLISH CHEESECAKE

A rich pastry case with a baked spicy cheesecake filling, topped with fresh fruit and cream.

COOK AT HIGH TEMP 210.

MAKES 25 CM/10 INCH CHEESECAKE

SWEET SHORTCRUST (PLAIN) PASTRY:
175 g/6 oz/1½ cups plain (all-purpose)
   flour
pinch of salt
90 g/3 oz/⅓ cup caster (superfine) sugar
90 g/3 oz/⅓ cup butter, slightly softened
3 egg yolks

FILLING:
350 g/12 oz/1½ cups full-fat soft cheese
3 eggs
60 g/2 oz/¼ cup butter, melted
175 g/6 oz/¾ cup caster (superfine) sugar
grated rind of 1 lemon
grated rind of ½ orange
½ tsp ground cinnamon
few drops of vanilla flavouring (extract)

TOPPING:
300 ml/½ pint/1¼ cups double (heavy)
   cream
selection of fresh fruits

1 To make the pastry, sift together the flour and salt on to a work surface (counter). Make a well in the centre and add the sugar, butter and egg yolks. Using the fingertips, pinch and work the ingredients together, then gradually work in the flour to give a

smooth pliable dough. Wrap in clingfilm (plastic wrap) or foil and chill for 1 hour.

2 Roll out the pastry carefully on a floured work surface (counter) and use to line either a deep 25 cm/10 inch round fluted flan tin (quiche pan) or a rectangular tin (pan), about 28 × 18 × 4 cm/11 × 7 × 1½ inches, lightly greased. Trim and crimp the edges.

3 To make the filling, beat the cheese until smooth, then beat in the eggs, butter, sugar, citrus rinds, cinnamon and vanilla. Spoon the cheese mixture into the pastry case (pie shell) and spread out evenly.

4 Bake in a preheated oven at 180°C/ 350°F/Gas Mark 4 for 50–60 minutes, until quite firm. Leave to cool in the tin (pan). The cheesecake will sink as it cools.

5 Whip the cream until thick, then spread a layer over the top of the cheesecake, marking attractively with a round-bladed knife. Put the remaining cream into a piping bag fitted with a star nozzle (tip). Decorate the cheesecake with piped cream and pieces of fresh fruit, and cut into squares or wedges to serve.

44

STEP 2

STEP 3

STEP 4

STEP 6

KUGELHUPF

This spicy cake mix is flavoured with orange and chopped ginger, and is baked in a special tall fluted ring mould, then drizzled with glacé icing (frosting). For an even richer flavour, add a tablespoon of the ginger syrup from the jar to the pouring syrup.

MAKES 18 CM/7 INCH CAKE

175 g/6 oz/³/₄ cup butter or margarine
175 g/6 oz/³/₄ cup caster (superfine) sugar
3 eggs
175 g/6 oz/1¹/₂ cups self-raising flour
60 g/2 oz/¹/₂ cup plain (all-purpose) flour
¹/₂ tsp ground allspice
1 tsp mixed (apple pie) spice
grated rind of 2 oranges
45 g/1¹/₂ oz/¹/₄ cup cut mixed (candied) peel
45 g/1¹/₂ oz/¹/₄ cup stem or glacé (candied)
   ginger, chopped
finely pared rind of 1 orange
60 g/2 oz/¹/₄ cup caster (superfine) sugar

SYRUP:
60 g/2 oz/¹/₂ cup icing (confectioners')
   sugar, sifted
4 tbsp orange juice

ICING (FROSTING):
125 g/4 oz/scant 1 cup icing
   (confectioners') sugar, sifted
1 tsp orange flower water

1 Grease a 1.5 litre/2³/₄ pint/7¹/₂ cup ring mould and dust with flour.

2 Cream together the butter and sugar until very light, fluffy and pale. Beat in the eggs one at a time, following each with a spoonful of the plain (all-purpose) flour. Sift the remaining flours together with the spices and fold into the mixture, followed by the grated orange rind, mixed (candied) peel, ginger and 1 tablespoon of cold water. Spoon into the mould and level the top.

3 Bake in a preheated oven at 180°C/350°F/Gas Mark 4 for 50–60 minutes, or until well risen and firm to the touch. Leave to cool briefly, then loosen and invert on a wire rack.

4 For the syrup, blend the sugar and orange juice and spoon over the warm cake. Leave to cool, then store in an airtight container for 24 hours.

5 Cut the orange rind into fine strips and put in a saucepan. Cover with water, add the sugar and simmer for 5 minutes until tender and syrupy. Drain.

6 To make the icing (frosting), put the sugar into a bowl with the orange flower water and enough tepid water to mix to a spreading consistency. Spread over the top of the cake, letting it run down the sides. Sprinkle with the orange strips and leave to set.

Gâteaux

A gâteau either makes an elaborate and attractive centrepiece for the dessert section of a buffet table or completes an elegant dinner party menu. It can also be served in small slices at a coffee morning or on any occasion when you would like to impress your guests. Gâteaux are not the quickest desserts to prepare because most of them require several individual recipes to be put together to make the finished dish, but provided you allow enough time, the result is always worthwhile both for the guests and the cook! The main advantage is that most gâteaux have to be assembled and often even completed well in advance, thus cutting down on the time needed for last-minute preparations. Many gâteaux can be frozen at one stage or another, and some can be completed and then frozen, needing only final decoration on thawing.

Experiment with different types and flavours of cake, use rich pastry, choux or meringue layers, and vary the type of butter cream to include the rich version or pastry cream – all of which can be used for fillings and toppings alike – and add a variety of fresh or canned fruits, chocolate formed into miniature curls, leaves and caraque, and a wide variety of nuts. And don't forget to add a touch of liqueur, rum, brandy or sherry – only a little is required, but what a difference it can make.

Opposite: A sumptuous gâteau is the perfect centrepiece for any meal, and can be served at teatime or after a special dinner in place of dessert.

STEP 2

STEP 3

STEP 4

STEP 5

SACHERTORTE

This rich chocolate gâteau was the invention of Franz Sacher who owned a hotel in Vienna in the 1880s. There are now many recipes that copy his speciality, and this is one of them.

MAKES 23CM/9 INCH CAKE

150 g/5 oz/5 squares dark chocolate
150 g/5 oz/²/₃ cup caster (superfine) sugar
150 g/5 oz/²/₃ cup butter
5 eggs, separated
few drops of vanilla flavouring (extract)
150 g/5 oz/1¼ cups plain (all-purpose)
*   flour*
1 tsp baking powder
300 g/10 oz/generous ³/₄ cup apricot jam,
*   sieved (strained)*
1 quantity Chocolate Butter Cream (see
*   page 79)*

CHOCOLATE ICING (FROSTING):
175 g/6 oz/6 squares dark chocolate
175 ml/6 fl oz/³/₄ cup water
good knob of butter
125 g/4 oz/½ cup caster (superfine) sugar

1 Grease a 23 cm/9 inch springform tin (pan) and line with non-stick baking parchment. Dust with flour. Melt the chocolate with 1 tablespoon water in a bowl over a pan of simmering water.

2 Cream the sugar and butter together until light and fluffy. Beat in the egg yolks one at a time, then beat in the melted chocolate and vanilla. Fold the sifted flour and baking powder into the mixture. Whisk the egg whites until very stiff and beat a tablespoonful into the mixture, then fold in the rest evenly.

3 Spoon the mixture into the lined tin (pan), level the top and bake in a preheated oven at 150°C/300°F/Gas Mark 2 for about 1 hour, or until well risen and firm. Cool in the tin (pan) for 3 minutes, then invert on a wire rack.

4 When it is cold, split the cake in half and spread with half the jam. Reassemble the cake and spread the remaining jam all over the cake.

5 To make the icing (frosting), melt the chocolate with 2 tablespoons of the water, as above. Stir in the butter until melted. Boil the remaining water with the sugar until syrupy (see page 76–7). Pour over the chocolate and beat until smooth. Leave to cool, beating occasionally, until thick enough to stick to the cake. Pour over the cake and spread to cover the sides and top evenly.

6 Use a piping bag and small star nozzle (tip) to pipe chocolate butter cream stars around the edge and base of the cake. Use a plain writing nozzle (tip) to write 'SACHER' across the top.

MALAKOFF GATEAU

A gâteau comprising boudoir biscuits (lady-fingers) soaked in milk flavoured with brandy and coffee and layered with a praline butter cream, the whole masked in whipped cream.

STEP 1

STEP 3

STEP 4

STEP 5

SERVES 8

90 g/ 3 oz/³/₄ cup blanched almonds, roughly
   chopped
250 g/8 oz/1 cup caster (superfine) sugar
175 g/6 oz/³/₄ cup butter
2 egg yolks
150 ml/¹/₄ pint/²/₃ cup milk
4 tbsp brandy or rum
2 tbsp coffee flavouring (extract) or
   extremely strong black coffee
about 40 boudoir biscuits or sponge fingers
   (lady-fingers)
300 ml/¹/₂ pint/ 1¹/₄ cups double (heavy)
   cream
1 tbsp milk

TO DECORATE:
strawberries, sliced
1 kiwi fruit, sliced

1 Gently heat the almonds and half the sugar in a saucepan until they turn a caramel colour, shaking the pan frequently. Do not over-brown. Pour quickly on to some baking parchment and leave to set in a solid block.

2 Line a 900g/2 lb loaf tin (pan) with non-stick baking parchment. Crush the almond caramel until powdery with a rolling pin.

3 Beat the butter until soft, then add the remaining sugar, and cream until light and fluffy. Beat in the egg yolks, followed by the crushed almonds.

4 Combine the milk, alcohol and coffee flavouring (extract). Arrange a layer of boudoir biscuits (lady-fingers) in the base of the lined tin (pan), sugared-side downwards, and sprinkle with 3 tablespoons of the milk mixture.

5 Spread with one third of the nut mixture, cover with a layer of biscuits (lady-fingers) and sprinkle with milk. Layer the rest of the nut mixture and biscuits (lady-fingers) soaked in milk to make 3 layers of the former and 4 of the latter. Press down evenly, cover with baking parchment and weight lightly. Chill for at least 12 hours.

6 Invert the gâteau on to a plate and peel off the paper. Whip the cream and milk together until just stiff. Use most of it to cover the gâteau; put the remainder into a piping bag fitted with a large star nozzle (tip) and pipe diagonal lines across the top. Mark wavy lines around the sides and add piped cream to the corners and sides. Decorate with sliced strawberries and kiwi fruit.

BLACK FOREST GATEAU

Layers of chocolate cake flavoured with Kirsch, sandwiched with cream and black cherries with chocolate coated sides and a cherry and chocolate top decoration.

STEP 4

STEP 5

STEP 5

STEP 6

SERVES 8–10

3 eggs
140 g/4¹⁄₂ oz/¹⁄₂ cup plus 1 tbsp caster (superfine) sugar
90 g/3 oz/³⁄₄ cup plain (all-purpose) flour
20 g/³⁄₄ oz/3 tbsp cocoa powder
450 ml/³⁄₄ pint /2 cups double (heavy) cream
90 g/3 oz/3 squares dark chocolate
3–4 tbsp Kirsch, brandy or other liqueur
1 quantity Chocolate Butter Cream (see page 79)

FILLING:
425 g/14 oz can of stoned (pitted) black cherries, drained and juice reserved
2 tsp arrowroot

1 Grease a deep 23 cm/9 inch cake tin (pan) and line with non-stick baking parchment. Whisk the eggs and sugar together until the mixture is very thick and pale in colour and the whisk leaves a heavy trail when lifted.

2 Sift the flour and cocoa powder together twice, then fold evenly and lightly through the mixture. Pour into the prepared tin (pan) and bake in a preheated oven at 190°C/375°F/Gas Mark 5 for about 30 minutes, or until well risen and firm to the touch. Invert on a wire rack and cool.

3 To make the filling, mix the cherries and 150 ml/¹⁄₄ pint/²⁄₃ cup of the juice with the arrowroot. Bring slowly to the boil, stirring continuously, and boil until clear and thickened. Reserve 8 cherries for decoration. Halve the rest and add to the sauce, then cool.

4 Whip the cream until thick enough to pipe and put 4 tablespoons into a piping bag with a large star nozzle (tip). Pare the chocolate into curls. Split the cake horizontally into 3 layers. Spread the first layer with some of the cream and half the cherry mixture.

5 Cover with the second cake layer, sprinkle with the liqueur, then spread with some of the butter cream and the remaining cherry mixture. Top with the final layer of cake. Cover the sides with the rest of the butter cream.

6 Spread the remaining whipped cream over the top of the gâteau and press the chocolate curls around the sides of the gâteau. Pipe 8 whirls of cream on the top. Add a cherry to each whirl. Chill for 2–3 hours.

ST HONORE GATEAU

A rich shortbread type of base topped with layers of choux pastry topped with caramel, with a pastry cream and fruit centre.

STEP 4

SERVES 8–10

1 quantity Flan Pastry (see page 77)
2 quantities Choux Paste (see page 22)
300 ml/¹/₂ pint/1¹/₄ cups double (heavy) cream
250 g/8 oz/2 cups caster (superfine) sugar
2 quantities Pastry Cream (see page 78)
425 g/14 oz can of apricot or peach halves, well drained
few pieces of angelica or blanched pistachio nuts to decorate (optional)

1 Grease 3 baking sheets or cover with non-stick baking parchment. Roll out the flan pastry to a 20 cm/8 inch circle and place on a baking sheet. Crimp the pastry edges and prick all over. Bake in a preheated oven at 180°C/350°F/Gas Mark 4 for about 20 minutes, or until lightly coloured and firm. Leave to cool, then transfer to a wire rack.

2 Put the choux paste into a piping bag with a 2 cm/³/₄ inch plain nozzle (tip) and pipe a 23 cm/9 inch ring on another baking sheet. Use the rest of the choux paste to pipe 14–18 walnut-sized choux balls on the remaining baking sheet. Bake in a preheated oven at 220°C/425°F/Gas Mark 7 for about 25 minutes, or until golden brown and firm.

3 Transfer the choux ring and buns to a wire rack and pierce the ring and each bun to let the steam escape. Leave to cool. Whip the cream and use most of it to fill the buns, putting the remainder into a piping bag fitted with a star nozzle (tip).

STEP 4

4 To make the caramel, heat the sugar gently in a heavy-based saucepan until liquid and then continue until golden brown; remove from the heat. Spread a little around the edge of the pastry circle and position the choux ring on top of it. Dip the tops of each choux bun in the caramel, holding with tongs. Add a touch of caramel to the bases and stick the buns around the top of the choux ring. Pour any extra caramel over the caramelized buns.

STEP 5

5 While the pastry cream is still just warm, pour into the centre of the choux ring. Brush the pastry cream with a little apricot juice from the can to prevent a skin forming and leave to set.

6 Arrange the apricot halves evenly over the pastry cream. Use the remaining whipped cream to pipe on a decoration, and add small pieces of angelica or blanched nuts, if liked.

STEP 6

STEP 4

STEP 5

STEP 6

STEP 6

ORANGE CARAQUE GATEAU

An oblong orange-flavoured cake with a rich orange filling, a masking of chocolate butter cream and a topping of caraque chocolate.

SERVES 8–10

175 g/6 oz/³/₄ cup butter or soft margarine
90 g/3 oz/¹/₃ cup caster (superfine) sugar
90 g/3 oz/¹/₂ cup light soft brown sugar
3 eggs
175 g/6 oz/1¹/₂ cups self-raising flour, sifted
grated rind of 1 large or 1¹/₂ small oranges
3 tbsp orange juice
4 tbsp orange-flavoured liqueur
1 quantity Orange Pastry Cream (see page 78–9)
1 tsp orange flower water
grated rind of ¹/₂–1 orange
250 g/8 oz/8 squares dark chocolate
1 quantity Chocolate Butter Cream (see page 79)
icing (confectioners') sugar for dredging

1 Grease a rectangular tin (pan), about 28 × 18 × 4 cm/11 × 7 × 1¹/₂ inches, and line with non-stick baking parchment. Make the cake as for Victoria Sandwich (Sponge Layer Cake) (see page 8), adding the orange rind and using 1 tablespoon of the orange juice instead of the water. Spoon into the tin (pan), level the top and bake in a preheated oven at 190°C/375°F/Gas Mark 5 for 25–30 minutes, or until well risen and firm to the touch.

2 Invert the cake on a wire rack and leave to cool, then peel off the baking parchment. Combine the remaining orange juice with the liqueur and sprinkle over the cake.

3 Simmer the orange pastry cream for 1 minute, then remove from the heat and beat in the orange flower water and orange rind. Cover with clingfilm (plastic wrap) and leave until cold.

4 Cut the cake in half lengthways to give 2 slabs and sandwich together with the orange pastry cream.

5 Use 90–125 g/3–4 oz/3–4 squares of the chocolate to make Miniature Chocolate Curls (see page 79). Use the remaining chocolate to make Chocolate Caraque (see page 79).

6 Cover the whole cake with the chocolate butter cream and then use the chocolate curls to cover the sides of the gâteau. Arrange the caraque along the top of the gâteau and then dust lightly with icing (confectioners') sugar before serving.

LINZERTORTE

A rich nutty pastry-latticed tart with a filling of fresh raspberries, raspberry jam and brandy.

STEP 1

STEP 3

STEP 4

STEP 5

SERVES 8

PASTRY:
175 g/6 oz/³/₄ cup butter or margarine
90 g/3 oz/¹/₃ cup caster (superfine) sugar
finely grated rind of 1 orange (optional)
1 egg
250 g/8 oz/2 cups plain (all-purpose) flour
¹/₂ tsp baking powder
³/₄ tsp mixed (apple pie) spice
60 g/2 oz/¹/₂ cup blanched almonds,
    walnuts or pecan nuts, finely chopped

FILLING:
250 g/8 oz/1¹/₂ cups fresh raspberries (or
    thawed, if frozen)
250 g/8 oz/²/₃ cup raspberry preserve
1–2 tbsp brandy (optional)
icing (confectioners') sugar for dredging

1 To make the pastry, cream the butter and sugar together until light and creamy, then beat in the orange rind, if using, and egg. Sift the flour with the baking powder and spice and work into the mixture, followed by the chopped nuts. Wrap in clingfilm (plastic wrap) or foil and chill for at least 45 minutes, or until firm.

2 Lightly grease a loose-based flan tin (quiche pan) or ring about 20 cm/ 8 inches in diameter. Combine the raspberries, jam and brandy, if using, carefully.

3 Roll out about two thirds of the pastry with great care, for it is very crumbly, and use to line the flan tin (quiche pan); trim and level the edges.

4 Spoon the raspberry mixture evenly into the pastry-lined tin (pan).

5 Roll out the remaining pastry and cut into narrow strips. Lay these strips evenly over the raspberry filling in a lattice design, attaching the ends to the flan case (pie shell). Bake in a preheated oven at 190°C/375°F/Gas Mark 5 for 40–50 minutes or until firm and a light golden brown.

6 Remove from the oven and leave until cold. Remove carefully from the flan tin (quiche pan) and place on a serving dish. Dredge evenly with sifted icing (confectioners') sugar and serve with whipped cream.

CHAPTER FIVE

Celebration Cakes

Most countries have their own special or traditional celebration cakes, many of which are made to mark a religious occasion. Because of the wide variety, it has been difficult to select just a few for this book.

Celebration cakes come in all shapes and sizes, rich and less rich, highly spiced or heavily fruited, iced or plain. I have chosen a small selection to cover traditional Christmas cakes – one covered in marzipan and royal icing (frosting), another with a topping of whole almonds in the form of a Dundee Cake, and the richly fruited yeasted loaf from Germany called Stollen that is served in thin slices; while the Fruit and Nut Ring is flavoured with nuts, apricots, prunes and other fruits, which are also used to make an attractive and colourful topping.

For Easter there is the less rich Simnel Cake with a layer of marzipan baked in the centre and its traditional distinctive marzipan topping, completed with eleven marzipan balls said to represent the disciples. Hallowe'en is another festival which is becoming increasingly popular, and this rich chocolate layer cake masked in white icing (frosting) lends itself beautifully to the typical Hallowe'en decorations of witches and pumpkins!

Opposite: *Serving a traditional cake is the perfect way to celebrate special occasions throughout the year, from Valentine's Day to Christmas.*

SIMNEL CAKE

This traditional Easter cake is a moderately rich fruit cake with a layer of marzipan baked in the centre and a marzipan decoration.

STEP 3

STEP 4

STEP 6

STEP 7

MAKES 18–20 CM/7–8 INCH CAKE

250 g/8 oz/2 cups plain (all-purpose) flour
pinch of salt
1 tsp ground cinnamon
$^1/_2$ tsp each ground allspice and nutmeg
175 g/6 oz/1 cup sultanas (golden raisins)
125 g/4 oz/$^2/_3$ cup currants
125 g/4 oz/$^2/_3$ cup raisins
60 g/2 oz/$^1/_3$ cup cut mixed (candied) peel
60 g/2 oz/$^1/_4$ cup glacé (candied) cherries,
   quartered, washed and dried
45 g/1$^1/_2$ oz/$^1/_4$ cup stem ginger, chopped
grated rind of 1 orange
175 g/6 oz/$^3/_4$ cup butter or margarine
175 g/6 oz/1 cup light soft brown sugar
3 eggs
1–2 tbsp orange juice
625 g/1$^1/_4$ lb marzipan (see page 78)
apricot jam

TO DECORATE:
marzipan daffodils (optional) (see page 79)

1 Line an 18–20 cm/7–8 inch round cake tin (pan) with a double layer of non-stick baking parchment.

2 Sift the flour, salt and spices into a bowl. Mix the dried fruits with the peel, cherries, ginger and orange rind.

3 Cream the fat and sugar together until light, fluffy and pale. Beat in the eggs one at a time following each with a spoonful of flour, then fold in the remaining flour, followed by the fruit mixture and orange juice. Spoon half the cake mixture evenly into the tin (pan).

4 Roll out one third of the marzipan to a circle the size of the tin (pan), lay over the mixture and cover with the remaining mixture. Tie several layers of newspaper around the tin (pan).

5 Bake in a preheated oven at 160°C/325°F/Gas Mark 3 for 2–2$^1/_2$ hours until the sides are just shrinking away from the tin (pan). Leave to cool for 10 minutes, then invert on to a wire rack and leave until completely cold.

6 Roll out half the marzipan into a circle to fit the cake and attach with jam. Decorate the edge and mark a criss-cross pattern with a knife.

7 Roll the remaining marzipan into 11 small balls and arrange around the edge. Complete with marzipan daffodils, if using, in the centre. Leave to set. Tie a yellow ribbon around the cake.

HALLOWE'EN DEVIL'S FOOD CAKE

A rich, dark chocolate layer cake, masked in a white frosting and decorated for Hallowe'en with witches and pumpkins.

STEP 1

STEP 4

STEP 5

STEP 6

MAKES 25 CM/10 INCH CAKE

90 g/3 oz/⅓ cup butter or soft margarine
125 g/4 oz/½ cup caster (superfine) sugar
150 g/5 oz/¾ cup light soft brown sugar
300 g/10 oz/2½ cups plain (all-purpose) flour
2 tsp bicarbonate of soda (baking soda)
2 tbsp cocoa powder
4 eggs
125 g/4 oz/4 squares dark chocolate, melted
1 tbsp black treacle (molasses)
1 tsp vanilla flavouring (extract)
200 ml/7 fl oz/scant 1 cup milk
1 quantity White (Boiled) Frosting (see page 76–7)

TO DECORATE:
125 g/4 oz marzipan (see page 78)
orange paste food colouring
black paste food colouring

1 Grease 3 × 25 cm/10 inch deep sandwich tins (layer pans) and line with non-stick baking parchment. Cream the butter and sugars until light and fluffy. Sift together the flour, bicarbonate of soda (baking soda) and cocoa powder.

2 Beat the eggs into the creamed mixture one at a time, following each with a spoonful of the flour mixture. Beat in the melted chocolate, treacle (molasses) and flavouring (extract).

3 Fold in the remaining flour, alternating with the milk, until smooth. Divide equally between the tins (pans) and level the tops. Bake in a preheated oven at 180°C/350°F/Gas Mark 4 for about 25–30 minutes, or until well risen and firm to the touch. Invert carefully on wire racks. Strip off the paper and leave to cool.

4 Colour two thirds of the marzipan orange and shape it into 8 small pumpkins and a larger one. Colour the remaining marzipan black.

5 Draw and cut out a template of a witch on a broomstick. Roll out the black marzipan, position the template and cut out 5–6 witches.

6 Use a little of the frosting to sandwich the cakes together and transfer to a plate or board. Use the remaining frosting to cover the whole cake, swirling it attractively before it sets. Attach the witches and pumpkins to decorate the cake and leave to set.

STEP 3

STEP 3

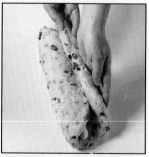

STEP 4

STEP 5

STOLLEN

This famous German cake or rich bread is popular at Christmas. It has a strip of marzipan baked in the centre, and is richly fruited, which makes it rise very slowly. When slightly stale, it is excellent sliced and toasted.

MAKES 30 CM/12 INCH LOAF

30 g/1 oz/1 cake fresh (compressed) yeast
   or 15 g/$\frac{1}{2}$ oz/1 tbsp dried yeast
2 tbsp warm water
90 g/3 oz/$\frac{1}{3}$ cup caster (superfine) sugar
6 tbsp warm milk
2 tbsp rum or brandy
$\frac{1}{2}$ tsp vanilla flavouring (extract)
425 g/14 oz/3$\frac{1}{2}$ cups plain (all-purpose)
   flour
pinch of salt
1 egg, beaten
150 g/5 oz/$\frac{2}{3}$ cup butter, diced
90 g/3 oz/$\frac{1}{2}$ cup raisins
60 g/2 oz/$\frac{1}{4}$ cup glacé (candied) cherries,
   chopped
60 g/2 oz/$\frac{1}{3}$ cup currants
30 g/1 oz/3 tbsp angelica, chopped
60 g/2 oz/$\frac{1}{3}$ cup cut mixed (candied) peel
45 g/1$\frac{1}{2}$ oz/$\frac{1}{4}$ cup flaked (slivered)
   almonds
125 g/4 oz white marzipan (see page 78)

1 Blend fresh yeast in the water. (For dried yeast, add 1 teaspoon of the sugar to the water and milk, sprinkle yeast on top and leave in a warm place until frothy.) Dissolve 60 g/2 oz/$\frac{1}{4}$ cup of the sugar in the milk. Add the rum, vanilla and yeast liquid.

2 Sift the flour and salt into a bowl and make a well in the centre. Add the yeast mixture, egg, 90 g/3 oz/$\frac{1}{3}$ cup of the butter, the dried fruits, peel and nuts. Mix to a dough and knead for 10 minutes, or for 4–5 minutes in an electric mixer with a dough hook. Cover with oiled clingfilm (plastic wrap). Put in a warm place for 2 hours to double in size.

3 Knock back (punch down) the dough and knead for 1 minute. Roll out into a 30 × 20 cm/12 × 8 inch shape. Melt the remaining butter, brush most of it over the dough, then sprinkle with the rest of the sugar. Roll the marzipan into a sausage shape the length of the dough and lay it down the centre.

4 Fold one long side of the dough over to cover the marzipan and then the other to overlap the first piece. Press together lightly and taper the ends slightly.

5 Place on a greased baking sheet, brush with melted butter and leave in a warm place until almost doubled in size. Bake in a preheated oven at 190°C/375°F/Gas Mark 5 for 45 minutes until risen and brown. Invert on to a wire rack and leave to cool.

AMERICAN FRUIT & NUT RING

For those who don't like marzipan and icing (frosting), this attractive Christmas cake is made with dried fruits, including prunes and apricots, together with rum and plenty of nuts, and has a glazed topping of glacé (candied) fruits and nuts.

STEP 1

MAKES 25 CM/10 INCH RING

175 g/6 oz/1 cup no-need-to-soak prunes
125 g/4 oz/²/₃ cup no-need-to-soak dried apricots
6–8 tbsp brown rum
175 g/6 oz/³/₄ cup butter or margarine
175 g/6 oz/1 cup dark soft brown sugar
3 eggs
250 g/8 oz/2 cups plain (all-purpose) flour
³/₄ tsp baking powder
³/₄ tsp ground allspice
¹/₂ tsp each ground ginger and cinnamon
125 g/4 oz/1 cup chopped mixed nuts
175 g/6 oz/1 cup raisins
90 g/3 oz/¹/₃ cup glacé (candied) cherries, quartered, washed and dried
grated rind of 1 orange
grated rind of 1 lemon
1 tbsp black treacle (molasses)

TOPPING:
about 5 tbsp apricot jam, sieved (strained)
selection of shelled mixed nuts
9 no-need-to-soak prunes
18 no-need-to-soak apricots
halved glacé (candied) cherries
glacé (candied) pineapple or ginger
angelica

1 Finely chop the dried fruit and soak in 4 tablespoons of the rum for 30

STEP 1

minutes. Line a 25 cm/10 inch springform cake tin (pan) fitted with a tubular base with non-stick baking parchment.

2 Cream the fat and sugar until light and fluffy. Beat in the eggs, one at a time, following each with a tablespoonful of the flour. Sift the rest of the flour with the baking powder and spices, and fold into the mixture. Add the rest of the ingredients, and the prunes and apricots with any excess rum, and mix evenly.

3 Spoon into the tin (pan), level the top and tie several layers of folded newspaper around the outside. Bake in a preheated oven at 150°C/300°F/ Gas Mark 2 for 1³/₄ hours, or until a skewer inserted in the cake comes out clean.

4 Leave the cake in the tin (pan) until cold, then remove carefully and peel off the lining paper. Pierce all over with a skewer and pour the remaining rum over the cake, then wrap securely in foil and store for up to a month.

5 Glaze the cake with some of the jam, then arrange the topping ingredients on top. Glaze again and leave to set.

STEP 3

STEP 5

STEP 1

STEP 3

STEP 4

STEP 5

CHRISTMAS CAKE

A really traditional rich fruit cake covered with marzipan and sugarpaste and decorated with marzipan Christmas trees and ribbons to give a seasonal effect. Sugarpaste can be bought ready-made.

MAKES 23 CM/9 INCH CAKE

23 cm/9 inch round fruit cake (see page 77)
using half the recipe quantity
1 kg/2 lb marzipan (see page 78)
silver balls to decorate
875 g/1¾ lb sugarpaste
125 g/4 oz/⅓ cup apricot jam, sieved
(strained) and mixed with 2 tbsp water
1.25 metres/1½ yards wide satin ribbon
⅓ quantity Royal Icing (see page 77)
green and red paste food colourings

1 Cover the cake with marzipan (see page 78), using 875 g/1¾ lb, and leave for 2–3 days to dry. Colour the remainder red and green and use to make 10 Christmas trees (see page 79). Decorate them with silver balls.

2 Attach the cake to a 30 cm/12 inch cake board with a dab of icing. Knead the sugarpaste until smooth. Roll out on baking parchment to a circle 15 cm/6 inches larger than the cake. Brush the marzipan lightly with the apricot glaze and position the sugarpaste over the cake.

3 Using fingers dipped in icing (confectioners') sugar, mould the sugarpaste to fit the cake, making sure

there are no air bubbles. Trim round the base. Use a smoothing tool, or your fingers and the side of a clean bottle, to roll the sides and top until smooth. Trim and leave to set.

4 Attach the ribbon over the cake with dabs of icing and pins. Half fill a piping bag fitted with a No. 2 plain writing nozzle (tip) with royal icing and pipe lines parallel to the ribbon at 1 cm/½ inch intervals to the edge of the cake. Repeat on the other side. Pipe across the first lines at right angles. Add a second line very close to the first, then leave a 1 cm/½ inch gap. Write 'Happy Christmas' between the ribbons, and, when dry, overpipe to make it stand out.

5 Fit a piping bag with a small star nozzle (tip) and fill with royal icing. Pipe a line of shells inside the ribbon and all round the top edge of the cake. Add a twisted coil of royal icing around the base to attach the cake to the board. Add 2 dots beneath alternate shells on the top edges and a series of stars on the sides. Attach 8 Christmas trees around the sides with a dab of royal icing and attach the last 2 on the top. Leave to dry.

STEP 1

STEP 2

STEP 4

STEP 5

DUNDEE CAKE

A good rich fruit cake with a traditional blanched almond topping that keeps really well. If liked, spike the top with a skewer and pour over 4–5 tablespoons of brandy before wrapping.

MAKES 20 CM/8 INCH CAKE

250 g/8 oz/1¹/₃ cups seedless raisins
125 g/4 oz/²/₃ cup stoned raisins
125 g/4 oz/²/₃ cup currants
150 g/5 oz/³/₄ cup sultanas (golden raisins)
125 g/4 oz/²/₃ cup cut mixed (candied) peel
60 g/2 oz/¹/₂ cup blanched almonds, finely
  chopped
grated rind of 1 orange
grated rind of 1 lemon
250 g/8 oz/2 cups plain (all-purpose) flour
1 tsp mixed (apple pie) spice
1 tsp ground cinnamon
generous pinch of ground nutmeg
250 g/8 oz/1 cup butter
250 g/8 oz/1¹/₃ cups light soft brown sugar
4 eggs
1 tbsp brandy, rum, orange or lemon juice
about 60 g/2 oz/¹/₂ cup whole blanched
  almonds to decorate

1 Grease a 20 cm/8 inch deep round cake tin (pan) and line with a double layer of non-stick baking parchment. Mix together the dried fruits, mixed (candied) peel, chopped almonds and grated fruit rinds.

2 Sift the flour and the spices into a bowl.

3 Cream the butter until soft, add the sugar, and cream together until very light and fluffy and pale in colour.

4 Beat in the eggs, one at a time, following each with a spoonful of the flour, then fold in the remaining flour, followed by the fruit mixture and brandy.

5 Spoon into the prepared tin (pan) and level the top. Arrange the whole almonds in circles all over the top of the cake, beginning at the outside and working into the centre. Tie several thicknesses of folded newspaper around the outside of the tin (pan).

6 Bake in a preheated oven at 150°C/300°F/Gas Mark 2 for about 3¹/₂ hours, or until a skewer inserted into the centre of the cake comes out clean. Leave to cool completely in the tin (pan).

7 When cold, remove carefully and wrap in foil until required.

MAKING CAKES

BUTTER CREAM
125 g/4 oz/¹/₂ cup butter or soft
margarine
250 g/8 oz/1³/₄ cups icing
(confectioners') sugar, sifted
few drops of vanilla flavouring
(extract)
1–2 tbsp milk

1. Beat the butter or margarine until soft, then cream in the sugar gradually. Add the vanilla flavouring (extract) and sufficient milk to give a fairly firm spreading consistency.

Variations:

Coffee: Omit the vanilla and replace 1 tablespoon of the milk with 1 tablespoon coffee flavouring (extract) or very strong black coffee.

Chocolate: Add either 30 g/ 1 oz/1 square melted chocolate or 2–3 tablespoons sifted cocoa powder. See also page 79.

Lemon or orange: Omit the vanilla and replace the milk with orange or lemon juice and the finely grated rind of 1 orange or lemon.

WHITE (BOILED) FROSTING
750 g/1¹/₂ lb/3 cups
granulated sugar
150 ml/¹/₄ pint/²/₃ cup water
pinch of cream of tartar
3 egg whites

1. Put the sugar and water into a large heavy-based saucepan and heat gently until the sugar has dissolved. Add the cream of

The most important point to remember when making cakes is to read the recipe carefully before you begin, then follow it accurately. Making cakes and decorating them is enjoyable and should cause you few problems provided you follow a few basic rules and guidelines.

Always follow one set of ingredient measurements, either all metric, all imperial or all cup measures; mixing the systems may cause the recipe to fail, as the conversions are not exact.

Cookers with fan ovens are a little hotter than conventional electric ovens, so it is necessary to adjust the temperature slightly. I suggest that where the recipe states 180°C/350°F, you lower the temperature to 160°C/325°F and check the cake at least 5 minutes before the suggested cooking time for a small one or 20–30 minutes for a large one. Lower all oven temperatures in the same way.

LINING CAKE TINS (PANS)
When baking a rich fruit cake, it is necessary to line the cake tin (pan) with a double thickness of non-stick baking parchment (which does not need greasing) to prevent the cake from over-browning and drying out during baking. Other cake mixtures need only a single thickness. Greased greaseproof paper can be used in place of baking parchment.

Cut one or two double strips of baking parchment long enough to go round the whole tin (pan) with a little extra for overlapping, and wide enough to come

2.5 cm/1 inch above the rim. Fold up the bottom edge of the strip about 2 cm/³/₄ inch and crease it firmly. Open the strip out and snip into it at 1 cm/¹/₂ inch intervals. This enables the paper to fit the inside of any shape of tin (pan).

Place the tin (pan) on a double thickness of baking parchment and draw around the base of it, then cut out just inside the line. Grease the inside of the tin (pan), position one circle of paper in the base and grease just around the edge. Put the long strips in around the inside of the tin (pan) with the cut edges spread out over the bottom (fold into corners with square or rectangular tins (pans)), press the strips against the sides of the tin (pan) and grease all over. Finally, position the second circle of paper in the base of the tin (pan) (which keeps the snipped edges of the band in place) and grease again.

To line a loaf tin (pan), cut a piece of baking parchment about 15 cm/6 inches larger than the base of the tin (pan). Place the tin (pan) on the paper and make a cut from each corner of the paper to the corner of the tin (pan). Grease the inside of the tin (pan) and put in the paper so that it fits neatly, overlapping the paper at the corners to give sharp angles. Brush with fat or oil. This method can also be used to line shallow rectangular tins (pans).

MAKING PAPER PIPING BAGS
Use either greaseproof paper or baking parchment for making piping bags, as follows:

1. Cut the paper into a 25 cm/10 inch square. Fold in half to make a triangle.

2. Fold in half again to make a smaller triangle and press the folds firmly.

3. Open out the smaller triangle and fold one of the bottom corners up to the central fold line, creasing firmly.

4. Continue to fold the bag over, creasing it firmly, to make a cone.

5. Either secure the join with some adhesive tape or fold the top point over twice to secure. Cut off the top of the bag and open out before inserting the nozzle (tip).

FLAN PASTRY
Makes a 23 cm/9 inch flan
150 g/5 oz/1¼ cups plain (all-purpose)
  flour
pinch of salt
90 g/3 oz/⅓ cup butter
1 tbsp caster (superfine) sugar
1 egg yolk
about 2–3 tsp cold water

1. Sift the flour and salt into a bowl and rub in the butter until the mixture resembles fine breadcrumbs. Stir in the sugar.

2. Mix the egg yolk with 1 tablespoon of the water and add to the dry ingredients with enough of the remaining water to mix to a firm pliable dough.

3. Wrap in foil or clingfilm (plastic wrap) and chill until required.

CHRISTMAS CAKE
Makes 23 cm/9 inch round cake
300 g/10 oz/2½ cups plain (all-purpose)
  flour
pinch of salt
2 tbsp cocoa powder
1½ tsp cinnamon
1 tsp mixed (apple pie) spice
generous pinch of ground nutmeg
500 g/1 lb/3 cups raisins
350 g/12 oz/2 cups sultanas (golden
  raisins)
250 g/8 oz/1⅓ cups currants
175 g/6 oz/¾ cup glacé (candied)
  cherries, halved, washed and dried
60 g/2 oz/⅓ cup cut mixed (candied)
  peel
125 g/4 oz/1 cup blanched almonds,
  chopped, or other chopped nuts
grated rind and juice of 1 lemon
grated rind and juice of 1 orange
250 g/8 oz/1 cup butter or margarine
250 g/8 oz/1⅓ cups dark soft brown
  sugar
4 eggs
1 tbsp black treacle (molasses)
3–4 tbsp brandy or rum

1. Grease a 23 cm/9 inch round cake tin (pan) and line with a double layer of baking parchment.

2. Sift the flour, salt, cocoa powder and spices together. Combine the dried fruits, glacé (candied) cherries, mixed (candied) peel, nuts and fruit rinds.

3. Cream the butter or margarine and sugar together until very light and fluffy. Beat in the eggs, one at a time, adding a tablespoonful of the flour mixture after

tartar. If you have one, place a sugar thermometer in the saucepan. Bring to the boil and boil until the sugar syrup reaches a temperature of 115°C/240°F, or until a small amount placed on a saucer makes a strand when rolled between finger and thumb.

2. Whisk the egg whites until very stiff. Pour the sugar syrup in a thin stream on to the egg whites, beating briskly all the time until standing in fairly firm peaks. Use at once.

ROYAL ICING
3 egg whites
about 750 g/1½ lb/5 cups
  icing (confectioners') sugar,
  sifted
1 tbsp lemon juice, strained
1–1½ tsp glycerine (optional)

1. Whisk the egg whites until frothy, but not at all stiff, then gradually beat in half the icing (confectioners') sugar.

2. Add the lemon juice and glycerine and gradually beat in the rest of the icing (confectioners') sugar, beating thoroughly after each addition until the icing stands in soft peaks. Cover the bowl with a damp cloth and place in an airtight container. Leave for 1–2 hours for any bubbles to come to the surface before using. The icing may be stored in an airtight plastic container for 4–5 days in a cool place.

Note: To colour royal icing, add either liquid or paste food colouring by dipping the tip of a cocktail stick (toothpick) into the colouring and then adding to the icing. Add the colouring in tiny amounts – it is easy to use too much and impossible to remove it! Beat well until evenly blended.

PASTRY CREAM
300 ml/¹/₂ pint/1¹/₄ cups milk
60 g/2 oz/4 tbsp caster
  (superfine) sugar
1 tbsp plain (all-purpose) flour,
  sifted
2 tbsp cornflour (cornstarch)
1 egg
1 egg yolk
few drops of vanilla flavouring
  (extract)
knob of butter

1. Heat the milk gently in a saucepan. Beat the sugar, flour, cornflour (cornstarch), egg and egg yolk together until quite smooth and creamy, then beat in a little of the hot milk. Return the mixture to the saucepan and cook gently, stirring all the time until the mixture thickens and just comes to the boil.

2. Add a few drops of vanilla and the butter, and heat gently for a minute longer. Turn into a bowl. Place a piece of wet baking parchment on the surface to prevent a skin forming.

each egg, then fold in the remaining flour mixture, followed by the treacle and lemon and orange juice.

4. Fold in the fruit mixture evenly and spoon into the tin (pan). Level the top. Tie a band of several thicknesses of folded newspaper around the outside of the tin (pan) for protection during cooking.

5. Bake in a preheated oven at 140°C/275°F/Gas Mark 1 for 1 hour. Reduce the temperature to 120°C/250°F/ Gas Mark ¹/₂ and cook for a further 2–2¹/₂ hours until firm and a skewer inserted in the centre comes out clean.

6. Leave to cool in the tin (pan); then remove and pierce all over the top of the cake with a skewer. Spoon the brandy or rum over the top of the cake, and when it has seeped in, wrap the cake completely in foil and leave for at least 2 weeks before decorating or eating.

NOTE: For an 18 cm/7 inch round cake use half the mixture. After the first hour's cooking, lower the temperature and continue for 1¹/₂–1³/₄ hours until cooked.

MARZIPAN
Makes 1 kg/2 lb
250 g/8 oz/1 cup caster (superfine)
  sugar
250 g/8 oz/1³/₄ cups icing
  (confectioners') sugar, sifted
500 g/1 lb/4 cups ground almonds
1 tsp lemon juice
few drops of almond flavouring (extract)
1 egg or 2 egg yolks, beaten

1. Combine the sugars and ground almonds in a bowl and make a well in the centre. Add the lemon juice, almond flavouring (extract) and enough egg to mix to a firm but pliable dough.

2. Transfer to a lightly sugared work surface (counter) and knead until just smooth. It can be wrapped in clingfilm (plastic wrap) or foil and stored for 2 days before use.

TO COVER A CAKE WITH MARZIPAN
1. Place almost half the marzipan on a sheet of baking parchment dredged lightly with icing (confectioners') sugar and roll out the marzipan evenly until it is a little larger than the top of the cake.

2. Cut out a circle or square about 1 cm/¹/₂ inch larger than the cake. Set aside. Roll out the remaining marzipan to a rectangle.

3. Cut two lengths of string, one the circumference of the cake and the other the exact height of the cake. Using the string as a guide, cut the marzipan into a strip or strips to fit the sides of the cake.

4. Place the cake on a board and glaze the sides with apricot glaze or thinned apricot preserve. Position the marzipan strips around the cake, pressing the ends together with a blunt knife to secure. Brush the top of the cake with apricot glaze and position the circle or square on top. Press the edges together with the blunt knife. If the marzipan seems moist, rub it with sifted icing (confectioners') sugar.

5. Leave to dry for at least 2 days. Brush off surplus icing (confectioners') sugar before adding the icing (frosting).

NOTE: If the cake is very uneven before you begin, first roll the top evenly with a rolling pin and then 'patch' it by filling in any dips with small pieces of marzipan, to make it neat and evenly shaped.

MARZIPAN CHRISTMAS TREES
Draw a pattern for a simple Christmas tree to the size required (about 4 cm/1^1/$_2$ inches) on a piece of stiff paper or card and cut out the shape. Using the pattern as a guide, cut out Christmas trees from thinly rolled out green marzipan (coloured with a dark green paste food colouring) and leave to dry.

A tub can be added, made from a small piece of red marzipan (coloured with Christmas red paste food colouring). To complete, add tiny silver or coloured balls to the tips of the branches with a dab of icing. Leave to dry.

MARZIPAN DAFFODILS
Colour about 60 g/2 oz marzipan a deep yellow daffodil colour with yellow paste or liquid food colouring.

Roll out the marzipan thinly, preferably on clean baking parchment. Either use a 5-petal metal flower cutter – about 3 cm/1^1/$_4$ inches across – or draw and cut out a template in thick paper. Place the cutter or template on the marzipan and cut out 8–10 daffodil bases. Use the remaining marzipan to cut out a similar number of 1.5 cm/^{1}/$_2$ inch circles. Bend these into a cup and attach to the centre of each daffodil. Leave to

dry, then using a fine paintbrush and orange paste or liquid food colouring paint around the rims of the centre of each flower.

MINIATURE CHOCOLATE CURLS
You will need a bar of chocolate and a potato peeler. Make sure the chocolate is not too cold, or the flakes will not peel off easily. Simply pare off curls with the potato peeler until you have enough. When made, they may be stored in an airtight container for several weeks.

CHOCOLATE CARAQUE
1. Melt about 125–175 g/4–6 oz/4–6 squares (or more if preferred) dark chocolate either in a bowl over a pan of gently simmering water or in a microwave oven on Full Power for about 45 seconds, taking care not to get any water into it. Stir gently until smooth and completely melted

2. Using a palette knife (spatula), spread the melted chocolate out thinly over a cool flat surface, such as marble, and leave until on the point of setting.

3. Either push a sharp knife held at an angle over the surface, scraping off long scrolls of chocolate. When it becomes too hard, melt the chocolate again, then repeat the process on a clean surface. It can take a little practice to get the angle of the knife just right. Alternatively, pare off the chocolate with a cheese slice. Store the caraque in a rigid container between layers of baking parchment in the refrigerator or other cool place for up to 2–3 weeks.

Variations:
For lemon- or orange-flavoured pastry cream, add the finely grated rind of 2 lemons or 1–2 oranges and a few drops of lemon flavouring (extract) or 1–2 tsp orange flower water.

For almond-flavoured pastry cream, add 45 g/1^1/$_2$ oz/^{1}/$_3$ cup ground almonds and ^{1}/$_2$ tsp almond flavouring (extract).

CHOCOLATE BUTTER CREAM
75 g/2^1/$_2$ oz/^{1}/$_4$ cup plus 1 tbsp
  caster (superfine) sugar
4 tbsp water
2 egg yolks
150 g/5 oz/^{2}/$_3$ cup butter,
  preferably unsalted and
  slightly softened
90 g/3 oz/3 squares dark
chocolate, melted

1. Heat the sugar and water in a small saucepan (with a sugar thermometer, if you have one) until the sugar dissolves, then boil rapidly until it reaches 107°C/225°F, or until a small amount placed on a saucer and rolled between finger and thumb forms a strand.

2. Put the egg yolks into a bowl and beat lightly. As soon as the syrup reaches the correct temperature, pour on to the egg yolks gradually, beating hard all the time. Continue to whisk until cold, then add the butter gradually, still beating all the time. Finally, add the melted chocolate until smoothly blended. Use at once.

INDEX